New
England Home

New England Home

Gloria M. Chartier

authorHOUSE®

AuthorHouse™
1663 Liberty Drive
Bloomington, IN 47403
www.authorhouse.com
Phone: 1-800-839-8640

First published by AuthorHouse   09/28/2011

ISBN: 978-1-4670-3633-7 (sc)
ISBN: 978-1-4670-3632-0 (ebk)

Library of Congress Control Number: 2011917438

Printed in the United States of America

Contents

EARLY YEARS

OUR FAMILY

THE SEASONS!

HAPPENINGS!

Thoughts on Faith

EARLY YEARS

Government Baby Book

My mother told the tale,
Of how one cannot raise a child
Without the baby book
The government sent in the mail.

It told her step by step
The way a mom should go,
In the baby book
The government told her so.

She followed it page by page
Of how a child to grow,
It was all a rage,
The government baby book.

It seemed to all make sense
And mom was so devout
But when my sister came
She threw the old book OUT!

—THE GOVERNMENT BABY Book—

First Home

The house on Plain street
Three rooms it had at first
That's all it had no more.
Dad added the bath and
A bedroom for me.
And then the rooms were four.

The fireplace Dad built
I wonder if it is still there?
He laid each red brick
And built the flue and
Chimney with careful care.

The place had been a tea room
A place for folks to come
To relax, eat and laugh
Dad and Mom made the place
A a sweet and lovely home.

Now I remember my Mom.
Dad grew a veggie plot
She canned and canned
From the garden there
It filled one fourth the lot.

Mom sewed so carefully
Before June was born
She was a sweet baby
So very small and dainty
Now many years a Mom.

Life there cut short
As divorce will do
I've not forgot the house
That house so small
My mind brings it to view.

It stands no more.
Someone tore it down
And built a bigger one you see.
But in my memory that house stands
That house will always be.

Plain Street

The house gone now
Sat in front of the lot
It was different then others
It had two gables on the roof
One "v'" separated by flat
And then the other.
The gables were there,
Just there.
Not leading or giving
Anything at all.
Just there.
They gave the house
The special look
That houses have
Which are different.
It was a yellow house
But hard to tell as the
Paint peeled in spots
And it has been years
Since I have seen it.
New owners changed the place
Spoiled it according
To my Mother
Who refused to ever
See the house again
And she didn't.
But it is special to me
And always will be
My early childhood home.
A place of safety
Within adult turmoil.

Honeysuckle

It grew in the back of the house
Profusely blooming in late spring
The Hummingbirds came
And suckled on the blooms.
The fragrance filled the air.
Seventy years almost
Has not dulled the odor.

My mother had planted it there
I think, but not sure.
Perhaps it was there when they
Bought the house.
I was so small I don't remember
They were there and I loved them
And although all is gone.
The memory remains.

Rusty Tricycle and Wagon

It was the depression-
I was just a child,
I unaware of the problem
That no money was about.
I saw a red wagon and tricycle
I wanted both like that
Full of vibrant color,
Red was shining nice.
I got them both you see
My tricycle and wagon
But color was all gone
And rusty brown, their lot
They worked so well
That I forgot the color
And just used them,
Like they were.
What fun!!

Little Grandma

Grandpa called her Clare
Her name was Clara
Dad called her Ma
I called her grandma.

She was not small
But not large,
In between
My Mom's Mom
Was large,
So Dad's Mom
Was "little Grandma"

She play "Authors"
With me and others
And taught us
"Jesus Loves Me"
And this I know.

She taught songs
She sang in homey voice
"Can a Little Child Like Me?"
And the words are still
There in my memory
So long ago
But I could still sing it
If asked.

A teacher before
Her marriage
So long ago
But she told tales

Of the big boys
And the switches
She never used
And chuckled
As she said it!

Gone so long now
Gone just before
My youngest son
Was born
Over 50
Years ago.
But alive still
And singing
In my memory!!

Big Grandma

Mom's mom
Was quite large
And not too tall
I guess she had
Been like that
All her life

She raised ten
Of thirteen children.
One still lives now
Ninety years strong
But the rest are gone
My mom included.

My mom was the tenth
The seventh that lived
One died before my mom
And if she had lived,
I wouldn't be me
It was that simple

She was a different grandma
Having so many children
Grandchildren were just that
Her kids children.
One or two were special but
Other wise we were
Just there, that simple.

She taught me to crochet,
And to knit
She did it so well.
I didn't want to
But learned some
I still don't do it.

She was my grandma
That's all-that simple.

Dad

So dark
So quick
In actions
Work and
Temper.
Life so short
So much fun
Laughter
Joy and sadness
He died too young
He would have
Enjoyed the family,
How it is grown.
Sad, but memory
Is a wonderful thing
He lives on
There!

Dad's Dad

Grandpa to me
And fourteen others.
Such a joy he was,
So small but quick
He played games
With me,
Hide and Seek
Back of the doors
Of the house
On Branch Street.
The dress he gave me
Was so beautiful
I thought.
He left it on the radio
When we weren't home.
I never knew him much
He died when I was four
But I adored him,
And adore him
To this day.

Mom

We mostly called her,
Mother
I don't know why,
But that is how
It was.
So dependent
Or so she thought
But did so much
In spite of illness
Which would
Never get better.
Worked hard,
Suffered much,
Loved the Lord,
And accomplished
What she began
In us
June and I.
She is gone now
As all others
But her love and caring
Goes on in my,
Heart!

Morn's Dad

Benjamin was his name,
A quiet man
A writer of songs.
He published one,
I have it still.
He wrote other
Poetry also,
I have copies
Of most of it
Perhaps,
I take after him.
Like his wife,
He never fussed
Over grandchildren
He was a quiet man,
And I wish,
I could have known
Him
Better.

Baby Sister

My sister, June
So much younger
That we hardly knew
One another,
Until we were grown.
Now as grandmothers
We are such good friends
And she doesn't mind
Being called "Baby sister"
NOW!

June

I remember
So well
When she was
Born.

Such a little thing
So angry was I
As I was told
She would be
My playmate,
But she grew
Became a pest
But now I love
Her so
My dear
June.

Branch Street

Grandpa and Grandma's house,
So dark but light with love.
So much happened there,
Music games and other fun.
All of their children,
Excelled in music.
Bruce was the one
Grandson who really
Excelled.
As a composer of
Many hymns and others.
Both grandpa and grandma died before
We, their grandchildren
Were totally grown.
With our children to share.
But the love of family
They gave us has
Carried through
All these years.

South Street

The other grandpa and grandma
They were called.
My mom's parents
Their large house.
Still standing on a knoll
By the side of a busy street.
A lovely home
So nicely kept.
However, they were
So distant.
They still are unknown to me
So distant with us their grandchildren
There were so many you know.
I lived in their house three years
And left and still didn't know
Them and felt they didn't
Care to know me either.
How terribly sad as they
Were good people you know
And so are we.

The Place on the Hill

I've been reading here this morning
I should have worked instead;
For the memories I've been thinking,
I thot long ago were dead.

I remember now a farmhouse,
A place so quiet and still
A place of joy and sadness,
A place upon a hill-

I remember the people, who lived there,
The folks of not so long ago
The people I loved and hated,
The people I grew to know.

I remember well my father
His hands are active still,
Tho far away from the farmhouse
The place upon the hill.

I remember his hands at work.
The hands all knarled but strong;
His touch never quite tender
But hands so far from wrong.

He worked from dawn to sunset
For many on many a year;
Had many on many a heartache,
Shed many on many a tear.

I remember if he remembers
Things my memory holds dear
The times he took me fishing,
    The kivers and my fear.

How well I remember the haying
Ah, the smell of the new mown hay.
The seat and hay-stained faces,
    For haying is never play.

I remember the furrows plowed
    The first year at the farm,
With Dad and Al at the pickax
They plowed the ground with arm.

Aunt Grace and I did follow
    Row by row with hoe
That's how we made out garden,
    In it our food to grow.

I remember the years that followed,
    The things from good to bad
The music, the fun, the hardships,
    And all the things we had.

How well I remember the drought
    The year the well dried up.
The water came from the end of the street
    And we treasured every cup.

I remember now Aunt Grace
    So short in stature she,
Of sturdy stuff this weathered one,
    As strong as any he.

With my Dad she kept in stride
Sometimes ahead one pace
It seems to me as I look back,
That she did run a race.

You never have seen one so swift,
So sure of hands and feet,
As Aunt Grace, with hands applied
To your un-mercy seat

I loved the summers there
With their golden days.
The blue Technicolor skies,
The sunsets all ablaze.

From my window I could see
The sky and the forest beyond the field of sod;
And who could but agree
It all belonged to God?

I remember my secret thinking place
T'was just a pile of logs,
As you go down the right-of-way
There alone between the bogs.

I'd go think good thots-sometimes bad,
Sometimes false-or true
But I'd come home a better girl
With a clearer point of view.
I remember the last time
I went there all alone.
The child I carried then
Is nearly eight years grown.

I wonder what happened to those logs
Guess they were sold for pulp,
They were in a quiet place
A place of Present Help.

I can remember how I hated work;
I'd rather sing, dream or reminisce,
Or just plain shirk-
Then shovel a load of dirt.

Now the farm is sold.
The house stands lone and drear,
My memory stands alone,
So unclouded; very clear.

I didn't know till now
How much I loved that place.
Every stick and every stone,
Every loved ones' face.

Perhaps we will together be
Where we will no more weep,
When there is no more toil and pain
We will sit at Jesus' feet.

But now the house is empty—
No one the place to keep
And as the poet said this morning
"Even the phoebes weep"

The Place on the Hill—Gone!

Hadn't been back for awhile,
To visit the place on the hill,
At least two years have passed
And we decided to go by
Where the old place stood.
Only to find it GONE!
Tom down and replaced
By what?
It isn't pretty,
Nor cute,
But a house
Like they build now
So large,
Quite ugly to me,
Not a warm home
Just a house,
Grand to someone.
Not me,
Even the hill is gone
Sad but
That's progress.

Gloria M. Chartier

New—New England Home

Gone so long-new home
New surroundings
Fifteen years
Is a long time
When you leave
Where you were born
And live so far away
From all you knew.
And then
To return
And learn again
What it is like
Near where you
Were born,
First winter hard,
Not used to all the cold
But the welcome warmth
Is felt when
Family near
Comes to
Gather!
Welcome home
New-New England
HOME!

OUR FAMILY

How It Began

I went to work,
He was there,
So young
And shy.
I, just eighteen
Just out of school
Life had been so
Hard for both
Of us
But here we were
And he asked
About me,
And was told
By a friend
And he came
And I wondered
How he knew
And he laughed.
We dated
One year it was
I left my
New school
And married him.
And now I'm old
And he is gone,
My true love
What a delight
To have known,
And loved him!

Bill

Just plain Bill
NO!
My love he was
For so long
Fifty five years
We had
It wasn't long
Enough,.
We needed more,
Gone for almost
Three years now
My husband and
My loving,
Friend!

Kids

We spoke of four
When we were
First wed.
We had three
And one was
Unexpected
As we had decided
There would be
Only two.
But so glad
And thankful
Am I
In my older
Years
For each
And every
One
Of
Them!

Fran

Frances Ann
Is she.
So very special.
Bill said,
"Boys only for me"
I am very thankful
God saw the need
To have a girl.
The first born
So very special
Even now
Although a
Grandma herself
She is very special
And I am very thankful
God gave her to me.

Scott

"No junior" Bill said
"And this boy will
Have a special name
Nevertheless."
His grandpa's first
And Dad's in the middle
Prescott William
And so it was and is.
There is now an namesake,
A junior, no less.
Not Bill's choice
But his son's.

Don

The unexpected one,
"You're aren't pregnant?"
The landlady said
As we moved into fresh paint.
"The paint will make you sick"
She said.
And so I was, so sick
The unexpected had happened.
Don was born.
Such a quiet baby,
Not so quiet child;
None of them were.
A busy home we had
All the time
Coming and going
Going and coming
In and out
Not only three
But the whole neighborhood
It seemed.

All Gone

He didn't mean to
They weren't important
To him.
Only a sheaf of
Papers
Not so big
So out to the trash \
They went.
And with them
All the verse
Of our children's
Childhood,
He didn't know
Or realize
How important
They were
To me
I can't
Reconstruct them
They are
All GONE!

A Thought

It was said to me by one
So bold-
"I don't want grandchildren
They'll make me old!"
My Chip-man then
Came in to view
Fifteen and one half
And six foot two!
He saysto me"
Gram look alive!
Give me your hand
And slap me five!"
I can't help but
Think
Chip
As you come to view
How young would
I be
IF
1 didn't
Have
YOU!!

THE SEASONS!

Icicles

I watched them grow,
Drip by drip
Line by line
The biggest one
About eight feet now
And growing.
The thaw will come
Warm by warm
Line by line
Until all are gone
Even the biggest one
Beauty exists in winter!

Snow

Intricate designs
With lacy patterns
Descend at oblique
Angles to the wind.

Nor'easter

They sought shelter in the Yew bush
As the sky spewed forth its white
A delight to behold
And really quite a sight,
Sparrows puffed up in size
It was such a nice surprise
To see them all huddled
A company snug and warm,
Against such an ugly storm.
Such love they showed
To one another
Friend by friend and
Brother by brother
None were lost as
They had each other.

Contrasts

The wind blew today,
Colors turned to parchment
In erratic flight-
Left geometric patterns
In places unneeded
On the lawn.
The herald has blown
His silent trumpet-
And these leaves
Of his command
Have held tenaciously
In what seems battle,
Only in the end to fall
And leave the sentinels naked.
Another trumpet sounds not quite silent,
And frigid blast of white and clear
Roar down and leave again design
And beauty upon the earth.
Thus it appears from my window.
The white covering the brown
Cold but warm to the earth\
Keeping the green under her blanket.
The clear glistening jewel-like
In the sun
Covering the sentinels and all else
After the blast.
From my window the beauty

Lies-
However deceptive to the touch. ·
The wind, the cold,
The white the clear-
Hold in keeping for a later time
The sleeping green.
The green-the promise
Which will come-
For it has been promised-
Warm, the resurrection
Again-of life,
Green and glowing colors.
Spring is sure.
It will come.
God is sure.
He will come.
The beautiful promise-
The hope of winter
Again-of life,
Green and glowing colors.
Spring is sure.
It will come.
God is sure.
He will come.
The beautiful promise
The hope of winter.

Contrasts Again

It was cold for the 3rd of May.
I stood than where
I sit now and wished for warm.
It is warm today-
As the 10th of May
Should be.
I wish for still warmer-
I think of the warm of summer.
The sun feels good it's been so cold.
Last week the wind blew harsh
The blue bond chill of the lake
Swept unmercifully
At my body.
I looked across the lake
To the pinks, greens and reds
Of budding trees.
The evergreens bowed and swayed
In gay greeting.
Today, May 10th
The lake ripples.
It hardly moves at all
As the winds in warmer glee
Fill the air.
The bushes nearby
In gentleness
Say "hello"
The wind caresses my soul.
I looked across the lake today
The static trees stand tall.
The same greens, pinks and reds
Stare at me.
Today, there is no greeting
Just beauty—
And warmer.

Winter Home

Glad to be home
Gone too long
Wintered south
Enjoyed it long
Home again,
Winter hard
Much snow
Covered ground,
Spring will come,
Hope will bloom
First winter home
Glad to be back!

A While Ago at Easter

I talked with Eunice today
Of things we ~ did and wore
A while ago at Easter
Of white shoes and gloves
And Easter dresses
Straw hats
With flowers and ribbons
Patent leather(plastic now)
And all the other trimmings
That made a girl a girl
A while ago at Easter.
A generation 'tween Eunice and I
Yet much the same
We share so much together,
Of all the girls
A while ago at Easter
White shoes and gloves
And Easter dresses
Organdy, ruffles
Pink and satin.
The dress up
Only a girl knew
A while ago at Easter
Easters come and go.
Special dresses still
Span the ads.
Yet not quite the same
As a girl I knew
A while ago at Easter.

Impatiens

She planted
Impatiens
In late April
I thought
It was too early
We had a cold,
Cold spring,
Colder then usual.
I walked by there
Today
And
There the
Multicolored blossoms
Saluted me
Bravely standing there-
Very patient.

Walk in Douglas

I like to walk in Douglas in the spring,
It is beautiful country.
The grasses are verdant,
Violets in bloom,
Lilac fragrances fills the air
Birds singing or on the wing.
This is country
Such as I knew
When I was young.
When you live in a busy place
Nature smells different
Sounds different too.
I like to walk in Douglas in the spring.
It is beautiful country.

Peace

Lanquid lake
Longing for
Summer.
Listlessly, lying
In serenity,
Peacefully
Lullin' in lullaby
Passerby (if they notice)
To
Peace.

Mr Red

Mr., Red and Cocky Proud
Was at my feeder
Again today.
His tip top ruff
Unruffled.
Eating sedately
Off the ground
While Sparrows
Chickadees, and Finches
Flitted about
With glee.
Eating their fill also.

Enigma

Gnarled, ancient
Apple tree, rotted
Inside to daylight.
Full of blossoms

Lilacs On Spring

A very large bush of lilacs
Bloomed so very near to the road
The blossoms fragrantly swaying
The bush bowed under the load.

I asked her if I could have two
I told her I had none of my own
I only wanted two of them
Not a large or burdensome load.

Her answer was NO
I have not enough
And people taking them
Makes my life so rough!

I had no intention of stealing
I only asked for two
I hope you remember I asked
You won't though
As someone had trampled through.

Line Rains

Line rains come
Says the farmer
To his wife.
Once past
They will
Bring falls
Change to
Life.
Line rains come
Says the farmer
To the soil.
Once past
The earth can
Rest again
And end it's
Summer's
Toil
Line rains come
Gives earth
A soaking blow.
And fore you
Know it
The earth
Is covered
With a winter's
Snow.

Line rains come
The winds blow
With a zing!
The earth is alive
It sprouts again
The earth
Again in
Spring
Line rains come
The earth is warmer
Still again
The crops grow
Green
And welcome
Back the
Summer!

Snow Again??????????

It's March, the 21st after all,
And it is snowing!
After a short nice thaw,
We have had at least six
Feet of the stuff!
Enough already!!

I know it is only March
But really six feet!!
We don't need more,
My car is tired of cleaning
As it cannot clean itself.
And scraping and sweeping
And shoveling is almost
More then a civil auto
Can bear!

Enough already!
And does the flakes
Floating down so nicely,
Care? Of course not!
They are free,
It is cold and so
They come!!
Enough already!!

It's the first day of spring,
Enough already!!
And still they silently
Come down,
Enough already!
Enough!!!!
And still they come.
Spring!!
Are you there?

Robin?

I thought you were a Robin
With it resplendent breast
Until unfurled wings
Revealed an Oriole
Baltimore at it's
Best!

Living

You haven't lived
Until you've
Stepped on a fresh
Cowflap—barefooted! !

A Bird

I saw a dead bird
On 95 this morning
I think it was a finch.
Small thoughts of sadness
Interrupted the rest
Of the day.

Campfire After Rain

Snizzle,Snizzle
Snit, Spit
Snizzle,Snizzle
Snit, Spit.
Snizzle, snizzle, Snizzle
Snit,
Snit, Snit
Spit.
Spit, nit, Spit, nit.
Glow, spit nit
Glow, Glow spit
Nit.
Glow, Glower
Snizzle, Spit
Glower, spark
Spit!
Glow, Roar, Spark
Spit.
Drip,Drop
Droppety, flood spit
Snizzle Spit
Snizzle Spit
Drip spit
Roar stop spit
Glow spit
Stop spit
STOP!

Gloria M. Chartier

Horseneck Massachusetts

4/20/86

The Rushing-Roaring
Crunching sound of pebbles
Rocks and stones
Being swept by the power
Of aqua green-bright blue
And darker green to black
Masses of water,
Brought to mind and soul
Fresh freedom
Yesterday!

Robins Fight!

Screams trill pierced
The air.
Not melodious
Or sweet-
As such you might
Find some birds do.
But tail to beak
Squack to wack
Darting and swooping
Chasing and screaming
Until the sight and sound
In the brush
Is lost.

Rustic Flames

Rustic flames
Leap through the forest
Engulfing all
Except the ever green
Forever
Blooming with
The
Many leaves
Of fall.

HAPPENINGS!

What Happened?

Jacks
Dates, School
Grades-life
Living!
Have they all come
to naught!
What has
Happened!
To all the sweet
Innocence of
Children!?

A Remembrance

4118/87

A church burned yesterday.
They said it was 180 years old.
I don't remember that far.
I only remember as a young girl
Taking solace
In a beautiful window
Jesus and the lambs.
It's gone now-tom down
What a tragedy-doesn't begin
To describe it!

Response to an Painting

The approach of anger.
The sense of thunder.
A crashing, angry thing
A blue black monster,
Descending upon a brown parched earth.
The woman bent before the wind
Lost in the noise and confusion.
A hateful way to end a drought!

Questions unanswerd!
Turmoil unknown.
Uncertainty!
Will the roof leak?
The roof hold?
A whole way of life
Seems to hang in the balance.
A hateful way to end a drought!

It causes a curious excitement
The power—the force of the storm
It causes swirling patterns
Caused by erupting dust.
Objects tom loose.

The Attack of the Paper

It waxed very strong throughout
The years.
The storage bins are full.
It's strength is growing
Day by day.
As garnered within the copy machine.
It has been quiet now
It has been quiet now
For decades.
But now the very distant
Roar is heard,
The march of attack is begun
And won't
Be beaten!
Pressing
Pressing
Comes the paper horde!
Like Alexander the Great
Enveloping all in its path.
People screaming
Machines whining to a halt.
Flooding, encompassing
Overflowing
Files
Desks
Chairs
People screaming
Till nothing is heard
Paper WILL triumph!
The battle is won!!
Quiet!
Paper banners
Wave
Very
High!

Opinion

I write a simple verse
And feel so stupid
When one so brilliant
Comes to read-a poet.
One so brilliant
Yet unabashed.

I write simple verse
And feel so stupid
When one so brilliant
Comes to read-a poet.

Yet again I ask
How does one
Become a simple poet
Without the simple verse?

If one becomes a poet—at all
It must be simply simple
At least
Once.

Opinion of a painting

Four shells, no more
Scattered in careless array;
With a piece of driftwood
Pointing to who knows what.
The sand
The sky
The feeling of the nautical.
Tho no sea, no gull
To fill the sky.
No sense of tide and time.
Just four shells, a piece of driftwood.
Sand and sky.
And then?
NOTHING!!

Old School

One room schoolhouse
Decrepit, shambles,
Almost departed-
100 years old or more
Stands disgraced now
But the drone
Of children
Still echoes from
It's open windows.
Days of rote remembered

Missy

Bill and dogs
So large that he
Didn't have to bend
Down to pat their head!
Now he is gone,
And so are his big dogs,
Missy is here
All eight pounds of her,
She with waggy tail
And shiny eye.
One eye is gone but
Her life is great
She sits on my lap
Or by my side
And bending
Down to pat
Isn't an option,
Eight pounds of love,
Joy and excitement!
Bill doesn't know
What he missed!

Bear Hill

I wondered why
They called it
Bear Hill
And then
I climbed
And climbed,
My engine purring
Nevertheless,
As it climbed the hill
On which I live now.
I hadn't realized it is all
A hill
Bear Hill,
Haven't seen
A bear though.
Wonder if they were ever here?

Two Horses

Two horses
In a paddock
Rump to rump
Nose to nose
Gossiping in
The
Wind!

THOUGHTS ON FAITH

To End—To Begin

It seems so strange to
To begin again anew
What wonders does the
Lord have for the
New Year?
Perhaps, He'll come
I hope so.

Sad?

I feel sad
upon the parting
Of such good friends
Until I remember
The gladder season
When we shall meet again
Jesus is coming
Then we shall rejoice!

It's Called My Lord and I

It seems so hard 0 Lord
To have to live to die
But there is hope
For all of us
It's called my Lord and I

A relationship so deep and strong
A bond so true and sure
That altho the world rocks
With wrong
It always is secure.

It seems so hard Lord
To have to live to die,
But we have in life a reason
It's called my Lord and I

God's Gifts

Another day
Begins anew
A present
Time
A gift
For you.

It is all
We have
This Day
Not two,
God's gift
For you.

Each day
So not
The same
That's true
Each day,
God's gift
For you.
\

The Magnified King

There is not a word to say
A verse to speak or tell
Of the glory of my Jesus
A Friend I know quite well.

The beauty of His person
The glories of His land
The streets of gold in heaven
Most above the mind of man.

I want to see my Jesus
I want to hold His hand
I want to live where He is
Even if His place is sand.

I know the place of Jesus
Is more then I can tell
My desire is on His heaven
But here to know Him well.

There is the Season

The color integrated
Mostly red and green
Mixed with blatant
Music softened
to a quieter note
Of tranquility, peace
And joy
Gives the season
A specialness
All it's own.

A season that is not a season.
A time that is not a time.
A celebration that is not a celebration.
For the season wasn't now.
For our time wasn't the time,
And the celebration wasn't celebrated
At least by all.

Christ Mass has come again.
The time we think of
Joy and presents,
Family, Friends and Parties.
The manger time
Jesus Christ in season.
Solomon spoke so long ago
Of time—
And seasons.
The time of Christ is now.
The season is now.
But not just for now
Forever.

They Were There!

Went to camp meeting
Spent the weekend
Looking at faces
That looked so
Familiar, yet
So strange.

Seeing folks I knew
In faces I didn't know
Sad inside and out
For so many
Gone, moved
Or died.

A sea of faces
To get to know
No strangers there
Just friends
Not met
Yet.

Jesus will return
Soon I know
There will be
No strangers
Just friends
There.

"Even so come, Lord Jesus!"

Gracious God

Gracious God
Who loves
Us all.
So much
He gave
His Son
To die
For each
And
Every one.
He gives
The rain,
The sun
The stars
And all
Of heaven
Emptied
For
Us!